Lovesongs For The Soul

A Spiritual Journey

Don V. Lax

BALBOA.
PRESS
A DIVISION OF HAY HOUSE

Photo Credits:
Images #1, 4 and 5 to Leilani Zerkle
Images #2, 6, 10 and the Back Cover Photo are by Desiree' K. DallaGuardia
Front Cover, images #3, 8 and 9 are by Don V Lax
Image #7 is by Morris Henry Lax

Balboa Press books may be ordered through booksellers or by contacting:

Balboa Press
A Division of Hay House
1663 Liberty Drive
Bloomington, IN 47403
www.balboapress.com
1-(877) 407-4847

Printed in the United States of America.

ISBN: 978-1-4525-8224-5 (sc)
ISBN: 978-1-4525-8225-2 (e)

Library of Congress Control Number: 2013916654

Balboa Press rev. date: 9/30/2013

These poetic offerings are a spiritual journal of my daily practice in the first half of the year 2013. Meditation, inner and outer cleansing, swimming and bodysurfing in the warm Maui ocean, and playing music every night at The Four Seasons Resort: these are the outward aspects of my life. The poems are reflections of the inner aspects...

It is my sincere wish that this book benefit all sentient beings everywhere.

I wish to dedicate this book of poetry to my family-
my mother, Patricia Macaughey Lax, who from early
childhood encouraged me to read and write poetry- my
father, Morris Henry Lax, who was a brilliant writer,
poet and linguist, and my two brothers, David and Peter,
without whom I would not be the person I've become.
I also bow to my spiritual family- my teachers and friends, and all
the spiritual beings past, present and future, who hold space for
the continuing evolution of humanity and this wonderful planet.

And, of course, none of this would be possible without the
Planet Earth Herself, for whom I devote my entire existence.

May All Beings Be Well,
May All Beings Be Happy,
Peace, Peace, Peace.

A breath...

A dream-

An awakening...

Ahhhhhhhh.

The journey unfolding

In this miraculous moment;

A gift of wonder-joy,

Heart broken wide open with tenderness

That feels Everything Everywhere All at Once

Resisting No Thing...

Rivers of tears that have no reason

But to flow back to the salty sea...

The soul-cleansing Deep Blue-

The Call of the Depths.

Grounding completely

In the agonizing awareness

Of our one soul's connectedness

Beyond the limits of skin,

Here------

we step into the dimension

Beyond dimensions,

Come full spiral,

And smile.

2.14.13

Time and again,

A merry whistler wandering-

Far and wide

His song to sing.

A root,

A tree,

A bud,

A blossom-

And a heart

Given whole

To the moon.

She found him by the sea,

And left him on a mountain,

And returned to find

The lingering fragrance

Of a smile.

Beyond thought

Or conjecture,

Beyond the borders

Built by words–

A little while,

Stay

In this heartland–

And silence may return us

To the true home

We have known

Was there

All along.

2.20.13

In the space

Where the wound was,

A scar, an emptiness,

A doorway---

Peer into that darkness;

Finding feelings

Of fear and beyond-

Willing to look deeper

Sensing all the way through-

There!

Breathing down

Into the sensation

Of falling into

The velvet star-specked Void;

So gentle and full,

Overwhelmingly everywhere

And now

Every cell is connected

To a star and

The distance between

Is filled

With music.

2.22.13

Diving deeper

Below the surface

Of this Dream,

To discover

The moment

Before Breath...

And in that space

When time stopped-

When the umbilical cord

To all that is

Was briefly blocked...

Finding the wall

My soul made out of stardust

To protect itself

From the wild, preverbal terror

Of separation from everything...

Understanding now

So well,

How I spent a lifetime

Painting that wall

With every bit of imagination possible

To create a universe of longing

For the True One

I'd lost.

And watching, at long, eternal last,

As this great, amazing edifice,

Dissolves back into stardust...

And all the starlight, beauty and joy

Of true cosmos

Comes streaming back in

To fill this finally empty vessel

With peace.

2.24.13

In the School of the Sea

Today,

The Great Whale Mind

Took me

And taught my heart

A thousand ways

To say:

"Joy of Swimming".

Then, listening well,

I learned

Ten thousand ways

To say:

"Beauty of light dancing in water".

After a while, my bones vibrating

And my whole being resonating

With The Song,

In silent prayer I asked

Permission to join,

To find a harmony.

Such a smile of happiness

In response!

Here We are Together,

Singing the one melody

That weaves its ever-changing thread

Through all the oceans,

Touching land and sky and the universe

With the love

That holds the wholeness

Of this planet intact.

One ecstatic emanation

Emerging from the endlessly expanding

Core of The Mother-

To reach for the central sun

And join again with our

Original Essence.

2.24.13

My Son

Has gone down

To explore the valley of war,

And perhaps speak of truce

With the lords of death.

He holds high the flame

Of his nine fiery planets.

The Light of his awareness

Penetrates all dimensions of darkness.

Protected by his Names,

He is Taran,

The wanderer and saint,

And the Goddess of Compassion;

He is Raj,

Wild Dervish who rules the Universe

With wisdom and benevolence.

He is Peter,

The Rock, the Poet

And the Architect of Dreams.

Steadfast in the Center

Of random chaotic occurrence;

Standing strong and calm

Through storm and drought;

Moving with the grace

And the Love of a million souls

Who freely grant him their full support...

He Breathes the Beauty of the Earth

And the Power of the Sky;

The rays of the Sun, Moon and Stars

Emanate from his eyes,

And his Great Heart Shines

A Beacon of Harmony to All.

2.25.13

Today

Is a new adventure:

I breathe in

The light of the morning,

And follow those gentle rays

As they warm my insides,

And expose

Any holding or pushing away

That may have occurred

During the dreams

Before dawn.

Quiet and serene,

My heart opens

To each miracle of life

That presents itself,

Without a judgment or even language,

But simple awareness

Of the moment arising

Out of chaos

Into form.

This music

That is dancing

Between the cells of my being,

Connecting me to everything-

Is such a sweet song

Unfolding effortlessly

And leading the

Unmistakable way

In to the magic

Of this

New day.

2.27.13

Photo Credit: Leilani Zerkle

Once,

There was left and right,

Good and bad,

Dark and light...

So many pairs of oppositions...

Now there simply seems to be

This gentle,

Passionate dance-

Like the tidal sway

Of heart and lungs,

Moving as effortlessly

As the moon-blessed sea

Between the boundless shores

Of our souls.

2.28.13

Curious

Today,

Like the mind

Of a baby whale...

Opening her huge eyes

On the newness of existence;

Exploring the sounds and sensations

Of Life itself,

All in the comfort

And safety

Of Mother's Deep Blue

Presence

And the Ocean's Absolute

Embrace.

Here is a great vibration,

Known in the bones

As a father song;

My smaller being fills

With oxygenated joy,

And a lovely sound arises

Through my being

In response.

Now there's a new feeling

Of buoyant support

As I'm lifted so gently

On mama's warm back

And I learn

The wild expression

Of launching myself

Beyond the known

In an ecstasy

Of passion and release.

We swim,

We float,

We dive

And rise again,

And each moment

Unfolds in perfection

As the magic

Of now.

3.1.13

The choice has been made

To Live Now

In the Abode Of The Open Heart.

With interest we see

How

This changes

Everything.

Morning meditations observe

Any obscurations

And follow down, and through

To the original wound,

And feel, to heal...

Each layer of scar tissue

Softening and opening

To this probing

Compassionate

Light.

As the archeology

Of awareness

Reveals all chambers

Of the soul–

Each door and window comes open,

Each curtain drawn back

And all the rays of color

From sun and moon and starshine

Flood the interior

With a newborn dance

That sings beauty and love

To all parts

Of existence.

Welcome here,

Friends, and strangers,

and difficulties...

The floor is swept clean,

The bed is soft

And the linens are fresh.

You may rest with me a while

In this healing abode

And when we are ready,

We will walk forth,

Refreshed.

3.2.13

Fearlessly,

Joyfully,

Compassionately,

Attending

With laser-pointed

Precision

To the tiniest knots and tangles

Left behind by

The sticky spider webs

Of ego's last attempts

To defend itself

From inevitable

Dissolution.

Released now

To fly directly

Into

The wild winds

Of reality...

Spreading wings wide

To embrace every passionate

Energy this universe

Has to offer-

Opening even more:

Beyond the known,

Beyond perception,

Beyond conception,

Until all that is

Pours through this vast vessel

And every voice

Of every being

Everywhere,

Sings

In One

Great

Song.

3.3.13

Now,

And yet again,

Forever,

I release you

And myself

Completely

From anything

And everything

That could

Or would

Or might have

Kept us

In any way

From absolute

Clarity

And truth.

That you may choose

To Be

With me,

Or my Brother,

Or yet

With another,

Is no longer

Of any consequence

Whatsoever.

May your Root

Deepen as far

As it possibly can,

Nourished by the crystal water

And darkest earth

Of full awareness.

May your leaves and branches

Grow and reach

Beyond every known possibility

Till every blossom

Of your full potential

Blooms

In the ultimate reunion

With all.

From all of my wide awake heart

I gift you freely,

And without reserve:

All the love that there is.

3.3.13

Open and empty;

Quiet:

Listening...

In the deepest depth

Of velvet, dark, starlit silence

At the center of everything,

There's a low, powerful

Hum,

From which all

Manifestation is born,

And into which

It will all return.

This song fills

Every space of my being

And leads me gently

Into the mystery

Of another day.

3.5.13

Lapis Blue

Shot through

With sparkles

Of starlight...

Crown open wide

To receive

The song of the sun,

Light beams dancing

Through the water,

Through my body

And my being,

Tuning my heart

To the music my soul

Has known

Forever.

Resonate, harmonize,

Vibrate in great

Reunion

With the earth

Herself,

With the whole solar

Array and

With the galaxies afar

And with all of our beloved

Sisters and brothers

Beyond the borders of the known.

Just one true breath

Opens the door

To this home

Of ultimate

Remembrance.

3.7.13

Rooting deep

Into the Earth's

Electromagnetic core,

And allowing my own center

To become congruent

With that inner space;

All channels open,

All awareness

Resting

In calm abiding

Within the womb

Of our primordial

Mother.

Bowing so deep with

Tears of gratitude for this home,

This beauty

And this

Wild infinitude

Of energy that reaches

Beyond the stars.

If for a moment

We allow ourselves to be

Totally yin,

Empty

And receptive,

Giving up everything-

Even the idea of being...

Then we are filled so full,

That the flood of joy

Will never

Ever

End.

3.8.13

Deep in the heart

Of your secret desire

Is a temple

Of love and great beauty.

In this sacred space,

You make your home-

In harmony with

All of existence.

Each morning

Brings the joy

Of awakening

To peace,

And the songs

Of sweet birds

Lead you gently

Into the day.

Each night

Brings the gentle sleep

Of dreams filled with light

And laughter,

And the magic

Of children

Dancing in circles,

Making rainbows.

Every afternoon

You give thanks again

For the gifts given freely

By a world that loves you deeply.

Resting now

In the absolute certainty

Of this true understanding,

You root like a tree

Into the Earth who is

Your Mother

And the branches of your soul

Grow up to the infinite sky

To bloom

A thousand flowers

Of happiness

With the fragrance of bliss

In the golden warmth

Of the sun.

3.9.13

We seem to have lost

The distinction

Between dimensions...

Dreams unfold

Into the day,

And morning opens

Like a flower

Into light.

Am I breathing underwater

Or dancing

Through the air?

Is this space between

The truth of being

Or are we somewhere

Completely beyond

Definition?

A friend asked

That I lead her soul

With a song,

Out of her dying body

And into a world of light.

When I listened within to the melody

That was calling her home

My own soul shifted

And my heart learned to hear

In a way it had never known.

Let this realm

Of divine mystery

Hold us all so gently

In the great womb

Of our original

Reality.

3.9.13

Emergent sacred patterns

Of scintillating

Living Light

Lead our essence

Effortlessly

To open doorways

Through the chambers

Of our unwinding spiral soul.

Outward and in,

Around and down,

Infinitely wide

And diamond-pointedly

Precise,

Awareness so tenderly explores

The vast expanse

Of this labyrinthine

Awakening Dance.

Holding and held,

Completely still

And attentive

To the tiniest detail,

With the patient care

And compassion

Of a mother who has known

Births and deaths beyond

Imagining,

We allow every wound to heal,

Every scar to reveal

Its own perfection,

And every lost particle

Of being to return

To the original geometry

Of ultimate

Harmony.

3.10.13

A quiet calm

Comes down

To enter

This opening-

Is it dark or light

Or some kind

Of new effulgence?

Full and empty,

Curious and alert-

Follow the song

That's leading

Now to the source

Of all songs.

3.11.13

Time to rest in

The fundamental root

Of the chord of this life.

Every part,

Every fractal,

Every overtone

Emerges in a natural

Series from this space.

No need to wonder

What comes

Or goes—

Just sit here

Silent

And planted

In the depth

Of awareness.

Such a curious enthusiasm

To witness

How this fern frond

Uncurls

In endless beauty.

So passionately in love

With every tone

And shade

And nuance

Of the song being sung to our souls...

Here is the music–

Now all that remains

Is the dance.

3.12.13

Resonant vibratory reality

Settles into the marrow

Of bones and being.

Sisters and brothers

Of the deep waters

And deep star-spaces

Call and respond

Around and through,

Until every cell,

Every crystalline spiral strand,

Is scintillating with awareness

And the unified field

Of dancing

Light.

And now

This light is alive,

Illuminating all

That's within

And around,

And shows the way

Into and between

Everything

(and even

Every no-thing)...

As the great mother

Of us all

Sings up and out

Of this absolutely empty/full

Vehicle of joy,

A gentle smile

Moves us

All the way

Through.

3.13.13

Photo Credit: Desiree' K. DallaGuardia

45

Carefully, Compassionately

Bringing the tightly closed

Flower bud

Into the warmth of morning sun-

Breathing on it,

Lightly watering

Its roots,

And observing,

With endless patient awareness

The process of unfurling.

Even so,

The story of these ancient imprints on our souls,

Laid over with ages of sedimentary

Scar tissue-

Requiring the finest

Archaeological acumen

To bring up and out

Every lost particle of true essence

From the frozen tundra

Of lifetimes without love.

And here, finally,

Like a warm afternoon in spring,

The river has found

Its song again,

And the meadow is fragrant

With a thousand blooming wildflowers

Returning at last

To the joy of emerging

Into a world

Miraculous

In its original

Conception.

3.14.13

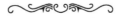

We are witnessing the end

Of the winter of this world-

The thaw has begun,

And mountain streams,

Locked for ages

In frozen solitude,

Are feeling the motion

And music

Of water

Again.

In the distance

A huge wild animal

With velvet fur

The color of night before dawn,

Lifts its head and roars

So loud

That all the bones

In our bodies

Tremble with the terror

And joy

Of passionate release.

Flocks of gloriously plumaged birds

Rise into the opening sky

And spread wings wide, wide to receive

All the gifts of the warming updrafts

Of earth's rebirth

From darkness.

In the deep blue light

Of this melting,

All wounds are now healed,

All judgments released,

And as the ice of millennia

Returns to its original

Liquidity,

The beauty within

Is revealed

To guide us onward

Into a land

Awakening to the season

Of Spring.

3.15.13

Time now

To investigate

The true shape

Of this soul...

Apparently formless

Yet supple and open

To respond to whatever

Arises in any

Given moment...

It seems closest

To the way

Water interacts with light,

And how they both embrace

Each other

And also co-exist

In permeable osmotic

Interpenetration...

And while they play together,

They welcome our bodies as well

Into the dance...

And with every ripple,

Sparkle, spiral wave

Or slow pavane~

We are learning from each other

And creating an architecture

Of dreams,

Manifesting new dimensions

And weaving new combinations,

Creating endless variations

Of color and beauty

Like the music of a great fugue

Rising through the arches

Of a cathedral

Into the stained~glass

Radiant dome

That echoes

Into infinity.

This then, seems the true direction-

To pay such exquisitely fine attention

To the details of the wondrous unfolding song,

That we no longer even know who is singing,

Yet are completely absorbed

By each breath

Emerging in perfect time

To create the greatest depth

Of harmony.

3.16.13

Lifetimes of dedication

To preserving and protecting

The power of the Goddess

With such passionate fervor-

Wondering now;

Were you seeking

Favor?

Unflinching willingness

To see the truth in all things-

Flensing this being

Down beyond the bone

To the marrow-

The pure and simple

Awareness

Existing without effort,

Without thought

Without direction...

Naked, exposed,

Floating in the wild

Sunlit sea of existence,

We allow our absolute emptiness

To be filled by the brilliant warmth

Of the infinite fire

That is the life

And love

Of this universe.

No questions necessary,

No answers needed—

Heart-valves operate

With the rhythms

Known forever,

And like the fluid

That is our

Basic nature,

We breathe

Easily

Into the next

Miraculous

Moment.

3.17.13

No desire

But to be present

With this precise

Moment.

Every aspect

Exposed,

Open to acute

Inspection.

So curious,

So interested

So wide awake

To know

Each most minute detail

Of the current

Situation.

What an adventure!

What a journey

To discover

The very foundation

Upon which

We've created

The intricate structure

Of this complexity...

And to find

That the fear;

The stark raving terror,

Primordial

And prebirth,

That left one gasping for breath-

Wasn't even one's own,

Belonged to another

Belonged to the mother

Who thought she might die

Or lose her child

Giving birth again.

And then,

To spend a lifetime

Holding the pain

Of ultimate separation,

And recreating

Again and again

This combination

Of holding a woman's fear

For her

So she might not have

to feel it

Or own it

Or ultimately heal it

Herself...

Now the dawn has come

And light returns,

As a baby is born

In complete

And absolute innocence~

Connected in every cell

To every star in the universe;

Grounded through ultimate connection

With terra firma,

Floating in the ultimate comfort

Of a vast warm ocean

Of awareness,

And knowing

Without any doubt whatsoever

That the Root Reality

Is Love.

3.19.13

There seems to be

This new feeling

Of twin vines

Twining up

A central tree,

Spiraling together

And apart,

Meeting at the root

And the heart

And the crown and again

Moving above and beyond,

Reaching all the way

To the light

At the moment

Awareness was born

From the Void.

Bathing in the deepest

Blue of blue depths,

Washed in whalesong,

Blessed by the Divine Presence

Of whale-mind,

Overjoyed to behold

The rapture of release

As these huge Buddha-beings

Offer themselves

From the water

To the sky.

All these energies

Within us and surrounding our souls

With the love of a world

Opening every eye

In every being

And every cell,

And every tiniest fractal

Particle of existence-

To the possibility

Of a new paradigm

Based on shared

Interwoven

Consciousness

That dances so gracefully

And without any effort whatsoever

Connects us all,

With gratitude,

In peace.

3.20.13

A gardenia flower

Has bloomed

In the garden of the heart.

Fresh and open,

Fragrant and wet

With morning dew,

Vibrant and alive

With a whiteness

That leads outward

And inward

To a center of gold.

Witnessing the essence

Of this Presence,

Completely suffused

By the reality ·

Of this perfume,

And gently warmed

By the rising sun;

My soul becomes evanescent,

And rises to join

With the great expanse

Of the sky.

High above the clouds,

Embracing and encompassing

The entire planet,

And joining that entirety

To the whole universe beyond–

Yet still resting in the sweetness

Of a small, heart-centered

Blossom–

Ahhhhhh...

This breath

Is all that there is.

3.21.13

So much gratitude

To this earth

Our Mother;

She's holding us all

So gently

So compassionately,

So completely free

Of judgment-

Even as we blindly thrash

In the birth-pangs

Of our own awareness,

Verging on mutual

Self-destruction...

Journey deeper:

Outward beyond all surfaces,

Inward beyond all depths,

Just allowing the energy

To lead us

Into deeper understanding-

Is it possible

That each and every

Exact experience

Of pain and pleasure,

Learning and growing,

Of each and every one of us,

Is simply an expression

And reflection

Of the actual

Original wound

And present healing

Of the entire Universe?

All of our anxieties

Returning to rest and

Realize

We never left home at all;

Our ultimate connection

Was never broken;

We have not

For one single instant

Been rejected or lost,

But here,

In this eternally evolving present,

We are still

So perfectly,

Precisely

And with absolute perseverance,

Loved.

3.22.13

Just this

One breath.

Pause...

Emptiness...

Feeling the space,

And what arises

Within it.

Following the line

Of resistance

Created before memory-

Down through layers

Of calcified

Sedimentary history.

Wondering why

This lingering rage

Protecting this persistent

Terror;

And discovering

The twist

In the knot

Formed when the soul

Sought to protect itself

From total

Annihilation.

A breath again,

Melting in

To the frozen place

Of lost awareness-

To find a crystal pure

Spring

Of Indestructible Innocence-

That's been here forever,

Waiting to be uncovered,

Rediscovered, Released, and Reclaimed.

Unwinding completely

Into the sweet essence

Of that water;

Bubbling up to the light,

Overflowing like a wild river of joy

To tumble out into the world,

Flying off the edge of infinity

Into the great void

Of ultimate possibility,

Giving birth

To entire landscapes

Of unimaginable beauty

And leading

Inevitably

Home

To the sea.

3.23.13

What does it mean

To live

In the Abode

Of the Open Heart?

Leap from the precipice

At the end of the universe,

Fall laughing,

Eyes and wings

Spread wide

To the upsurge

Of wildness and beauty.

Breathing in everything

Without even the trace

Of resistance;

Breathing out tenderness,

Compassion,

And the love

Coming straight through

From the source-

Embracing everyone

In every realm

With unequivocal acceptance.

Then, so carefully,

Reverently paying

The utmost attention

To each most minute detail,

Preparing an excellent

Meal, and cup of tea

To deeply nourish the souls

Of whatever random guests

Have chosen this moment

To appear.

3.24.13

Silence.

Dark and soft,

Like the midnight sky seen

From as high a mountain

As you can possibly imagine...

And then,

From far off

In the distant light

Of a dream of sunrise,

Comes a chord beyond comprehension...

So deep,

So vast,

So all-encompassing,

That you know

Somehow

That all creation

Began

With this very sound-

That it lives inside you,

In every cell,

And that every atom

Of manifested existence

Is a note

Given birth

By that original

Music.

Listen now

With the avid attention

Of our entire souls

And we will see

The patterns of light

Emerging

From this

Ever-expanding

Symphony.

How our DNA

Dances

In a spiraling fractal

Mandala

Of interwoven star-dust,

And all of this evolving whirl

Has its harmonic root in

And inevitable return

To that first

Burst

Of audible awareness.

What now

Is there

But the tending and tuning

Of our hearts,

To learn the only song

We could ever know-

And to sing it so well,

With so much passion

And love

That all of us return

To the ultimate grace

Of perfect

Harmony.

3.25.13

All that I desire

Is to swim next to you

Through the deep sea

Of life-

Bodies moving

In harmony,

Hearts and souls

Open to receive

All the miraculous magic

Of each unfolding moment;

Minds quietly

Awake, aware,

And at peace.

Our breath pumps

Our limbs in synchrony

And each motion one makes

Is reflected

By the beauty of the other.

Sunbeams dance with us

Through the water,

Showing our enchanted eyes

The tiniest details

Of oceanic existence.

A thousand whales sing their great song

That holds intact

The very vibration

Of our world,

And our beings

Merge again

Into their original essence,

And melt into the union

Of our one

Undivided

Soul.

3.30.13

Infinity

And Eternity

Find each other

In a dream of beauty,

Beyond the known or any

Previous concept

Of Reality.

A motion of light

Like the wind

On Water,

Joins two dimensions

That otherwise might

Never have met-

And in the random

Intersection

Of multiple possible outcomes,

The place we choose

Is alive

With destiny.

Follow this music

To the source

Of melody,

And we will find our hearts.

In that space

A bright energy

Moves without motion

And time stops...

Even as the breath

Becomes still,

And the mind,

Quiet.

As we rest,

Before motion

Takes us again

Into the ever-expanding

Spiral of existence,

We know

Beyond knowing,

That this

Is the pure land called

True nature.

4.1.13

Into the vast, open space

Of the compassionate heart,

Breathe everything,

Without judgment or name,

Through every pore of this body,

From every corner of the universe,

Breathe it all in,

Barring nothing...

And resting with that

Great inclusion,

Allowing the love

That is our nature

To make the magic

Alchemical

Transfiguration

Of chaos

Into beauty–

Then-

From that same immensity-

That same well

Of blessing, healing and forgiveness

That lives in our center

But doesn't belong to us at all...

Radiate out again,

Through every possible permeability

Of our being,

The light that is the remedy

For everything,

The song that soothes every soul,

The sweetness that satisfies

Every hunger,

The truth

That settles

All doubt.

In this way,

Through simple

Opening

And breath,

We purify ourselves,

The planet,

And everything.

4.3.13

Wonderful stillness:

The quiet space

Between breaths

That goes on forever

And is full of a certain

Tangible light.

From this place

Awareness explores

Through the being

In this body, curious

About everything,

Simply fascinated

By the million multifaceted

Diamonds of possibility

Presented by every moment

In this life.

Silence

Gives birth

To music—

And the emerging song

Takes us on a journey

Through dreamlands of beauty

Where we find, finally,

The simple perfection

Of our well-tuned souls.

4.4.13

Let us now

Discover the beauty

And magic

Of this day...

What a miracle

To sense

The world

In all of its

Multidimensional

Wonder!

A breath-

A smell-

A taste-

A vision-

A rest-

To feel

Just being here

In a body

On the planet

Floating in space.

What greater

Perfection is there

Than this?

4.7.13

Our Mother,

This Earth

That gave us birth,

And Who is now

Rebirthing Herself-

Requires of us

A certain

Reciprocity...

Could we please

Feel

Her pain?

This pain in our hearts,

Our minds and bodies,

That we've carried

From life to life

And through death

To the next round again-

Because it's imprinted

On our very souls...

Isn't it clear?

She is ready to heal.

Are we willing?

Really, truly, completely

Willing

To go all the way;

To just give up

Everything...

Let go of the whole

Wild masquerade?

That we could

So fool ourselves

Into believing

For even one breath

That we are in any way

Separate

From her???

It's all true.

Without judgment or blame,

And with the greatest possible

Care and compassion,

Every bit

Of suffering,

Rape, torture and death

Perpetrated on this planet,

Needs to be felt

All the way through

Till we are finally free.

There is No Transcending,

No avoidance,

No denial

Possible.

Will we stand together now

And burn at the stake

Of truth

Till the last vestiges

Of vertiginous grasping

Have become ash,

And this self-involved

Group delusion

Has finally

Dissolved?

Please say yes.

Please let us

Walk hand-in-hand

With our Mother

And each other

Into a world

Where each of us

Can live

With the total

Trust,

Tenderness

And wide-open wonder

Of a newborn baby

Given birth

By Love.

4.8.13

With finest attention

To tiniest detail,

We look

Deep into the heart-

Behind the space there's a curtain,

Behind the curtain a window,

And through that opening,

We can fly.

Let us hold hands

And leap together

Into the great adventure

Beyond the veils

Of past, present and future-

Into the eternal moment

That stretches all the way

To infinity.

Do not doubt that we are held,

As I am holding you now—

In the great compassionate arms

Of the Mother of us all.

Each small flower

Of pain or pleasure

That we might find

In this garden

Leads back to the great tree

That grows

From forever

To eternity.

And there is not one place

On that tree

That is not

Your true home.

Rest here with me,

For a while-

As our souls

Return to their

Original

Immaculate

Essence.

4.9.13

In a moment

Of death and rebirth,

Let us give our awareness

To the breath,

And to the heartbeat,

And then-

To the magic that arises

From allowing the universe

To reveal itself

Unimpeded

By thought or preconception.

We want so desperately

To create a ground,

A controllable environment...

Somewhere safe

From obvious entropy

And chaos.

What if all we really need

Is our own

Inner quiet,

And an open-ness to whatever

The next miracle might be?

Perhaps this, then

Is the path we must follow

Into the constantly

Unfolding now...

With eyes, mind,

Heart and soul

Wide open and ready to receive

All the love

And abundant generosity

Of a perfectly compassionate

Existence.

4.10.13

There's a dark open space

At the back of our brains-

Let's just

Let go

And dive through it,

With that wild sense

Of rapture

You get

When embarking

On a new adventure

Into the completely

Unknowable

Unknown.

At dawn today,

We were drifting through

The sentient, starlit void,

And lights

Began appearing

Like beacons

In the form of archetypal

Glyphs of truth,

Each one a dazzling

Never-seen-before

Color,

And each one

A magic key

To open a hidden door

In the depths

Of our souls.

With all of our senses

Awake,

We tasted each enchantment,

And as all of the chambers within

Were opened,

A thousand multidimensional

Butterflies

Were released

To fly up

To the highest heaven

And take their place

With the stars.

4.11.13

Sometimes,

You just have to go

Down,

As far as you can,

Just letting

The bottom drop out,

And falling through

Without a thought

Of holding on to anything,

Or being caught

By anyone,

Or even

Having the vaguest idea

Of what

The outcome might be.

Suddenly all this

Solidity

Starts to blur

And lose its

Usual definition.

Nothing

To pin

Our hopes on...

No place

To reassure our

Little brains...

Not a single concept

That would make sense

Out of all this confusion

And chaotic

Reality.

Just this

Weightless journey,

Downwards,

Outwards,

Beyond the beyond,

Into the unknowable expanse

Of our own True Being.

What's left

After all that's unessential

Has been stripped away?

Such an ocean

Of light and music!

Dancing so subtly

With each other,

We turn about

The inner core

That has held us

Forever

In the perfection

Of love.

4.12.13

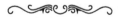

An old song

Took my hand and led me

Back to a time

Before the birth

Of science,

When the old magic

Still reigned

On Earth.

Dancing in time

To the seasons,

We circled together

For the joy of feeling our feet

Move with the rhythm of our breath

And the melodies of our hearts.

This is a music

Born of light,

That moves in us

Like sky-swept birds,

Swooping and diving

In spirals of ecstatic longing

For the sun.

We give ourselves completely

To the motion of our senses,

And open

All of ourselves

To the great unity of our souls

That sing

So effortlessly, in tune

With the Mother's

Great

Primal

Chord of beauty.

4.13.13

What new territory

Will we explore

With our awareness?

A tiny quantum

Wormhole

Into multiple universes of wonder and delight?

Or the deep red of a rose

That has appeared

In the center of this heart,

With a fragrance so powerful,

Every sentient soul

In all dimensions

Is suddenly

Slightly

Giddy

With joy

And relief.

Each day

Brings a new adventure,

Into and through

Every aspect of living

As a spirit

In a realm of matter,

Energy, space and time.

Somehow, it's becoming impossible

To label

Anything, anymore...

Just observing now

The play of light

Dancing in the depths

Of the great

Blue

Sea.

4.14.13

Shall we

Feel the fullness

Of our desire?

All the way through

To the fire

That burns hot

In every cell

For the Beloved?

And can we stay here

In the heat,

In the flames

Of passion,

And just keep looking

Deeply

Into each other's open eyes-

Till we fall through

Into oneness,

And know

In our bones,

That this Love

Has absorbed us,

Like the alchemist

Melting lead in a crucible,

Till all that is left

Has turned into

Gold.

4.15.13

Would you like

To be at the effect

Of some news-monger's

Attempts

At media-manipulation?

Or maybe it's time

To feel

All the way deep

Into your own

Original

Terror and rage...

Because, after all,

Let's face the facts–

This whole show

Began inside...

The outside is just

One

Big-screen TV.

Where exactly

Do you wish to place

Your full attention?

On the Big Truth-

Or on the Big Lie?

Do people really need

To keep suffering

And dying needlessly

To support our deep need

To remain numb

And ignorant?

So here-

Let's try something new-

Like sitting in a circle,

Holding hands,

Without drugs or alcohol,

Nor religion,

Nor mass-hypnosis...

Just the real,

Heartfelt wish

To Heal Everything

Down to the Very Core,

Right Now.

And if

We were to take

One breath together

All the way into our bellies,

And then

Take a good look

At what we're really holding in there...

How about now–

We take another breath,

Feeling it through–

All the way through,

Not passing by

A single iota

Of awareness,

Not shutting down for

Even the slightest instant...

Yes–

This is the path

To awakening

From the mad-matrix nightmare.

Will you all please

Join me

Now?

4.16.13

Temple bells

Are calling us

Into the gentle space,

The quiet place,

The dark and empty

Star filled

Wonderland

That lies

Just the other side

Of the busy,

Busy

Mind.

A breeze blows,

The bells ring,

We sit

In silence.

Just for a while-

To feel

The deeper reality

That's been waiting

So patiently

Forever

Just to have,

Finally,

Our true,

Undivided,

Naked

Attention.

So we listen,

And hear

Every song and sound

And thought

And quivering insect antenna

And hummingbird wing

Of this whole

Burgeoning planet-

One huge symphony

In which we are painfully aware

Of each separate note...

And then we breathe

With the effortless task

Of finding the one true melody

That will create

A resonant Harmony

For this entire

Emerging Earth...

And then-

We sing.

4.17.13

Greeting the day

With wonder

And curiosity...

Breathing it all in

Through every pore,

Until every cell

Is vibrating

With ecstatic electricity.

This magic

Is so easy and effortless-

Like a big sea turtle

Floating up to the surface...

Knowing,

Beyond even the existence of doubt,

That it will be

Where it needs to be

When it needs to be there...

So let us walk

A while in wonder

At each step

Through a world

Filled with the tiniest miracles,

Breathing it all in,

Until inside

And outside

Are one.

4.18.13

Such a fascinating journey,

Down to the depths,

Through the darkness,

Feeling with every sense

And a million

Unimaginable

Senses...

To know everything

In every hidden layer

And just accept it all,

Loving the whole

Wildly outrageous

Experience.

Dying now

With the overwhelming

Beauty of light

Dancing through

All the interwoven particles

That were once this body.

And finally

Just being so quietly

Present, Full, Rooted

Deep into the Earth

That holds us

So eternally compassionate

In her exquisite embrace.

4.20.13

A planet

Full of pain

And pleasure-

And just how

Do we participate?

Perhaps it's best

Just to be

Like the ocean,

Moving with the motion

Of the moon-swept tides,

Allowing the wind

To go wild on the surface

While remaining

Completely still,

Below.

All the while,

This water

That is the substance

Of our souls, is suffused

By a never-ending dance

Of intelligent light.

Listening closely,

We might hear

The music

In that movement,

And recognize the song

That leads inevitably

Home.

4.20.13

There is a music

We can hear

In the light

That dances on water,

And in the water itself,

As it moves

Through the seeming solidity

Of earth-bound

Appearances.

Listen!

It is singing

In our blood,

And in our bones

And in the very air

Occupying all the emptiness

That is filling the space

Within us...

So much beauty

In every breath,

And all that we need

Could be so easily granted

By the tiniest

Moment

Of silent,

Appreciative

Attention.

4.21.13

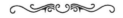

The little details

Of our lives

Are doorways

Into deeper awareness-

And as we step

With attention and care

Across the threshold

Into the minutiae

Of the Now,

The whole universe

Comes so clearly

Into brilliant focus

And beauty.

4.23.13

There is no time

But this moment

To bring into

Being

The true form

Of every aspect

Arising from the multidimensional

Fractal spiral

That is the individuated

Soul consciousness

Of our

Awareness.

In simple terms this means-

Be the truth

Of who we are.

Live in the world

As clear

Manifestations

Of our inner beauty-

Nothing held back,

Nothing to hide,

Nothing denied-

Just

Bare Naked

Honest

Open

Reality.

If we want this world

To reflect the outrageous

Possibilities

Of our deepest dreams-

Then we must be

Totally Willing

To pull the rug

Out from under ourselves

And dance

In the open space

Of Absolute

Trust.

4.24.13

Photo Credit: Leilani Zerkle

Like the Moon,

In full reflection

Of the sun's unlimited light,

Can we now be the perfection

Of this precise connection

Between space, time, awareness

And perception?

No resistance,

No seeking or holding on,

No pre-conception,

Nor any thought-form...

Just this naked, achingly open

Acceptance

With a passionate attention

To every light-limned detail

Of true-reality's

Ever-present beauty.

Each and every one of us

Adding our un-dimmed view

To this great, vibrating

Network of light that grows through our uniting hearts

To encompass this world

And heal every part

Of the universe we were born

To serve.

4.25.13

Open to all

Present possibilities,

Resting

In the warmth

Of the Great Mother's

Loving arms...

What an amazing view!

4.26.13

Will you join me

As we join

Within ourselves

The left and right,

God and Goddess

Dark and Light-

And Finally welcome home

This Universe full of unloved,

Uncomfortable, and unaccepted,

Lonely fragments

Of our own true souls?

It's not

An easy journey, but

Is there anything more important

Than healing everything now

That needs to heal

So that maybe,

Just maybe,

Our grandchildren

Might be born into a world

Of hope and beauty,

And find some portion

Of that primordial

Innocence

That was lost

So long ago.

Here's my hand, friend,

Take courage

From our dedication

To this unfolding path

Of open awareness-

And let us make the existential

Quantum leap

From this shrinking fear-based fortress of falsehood

To the great expanding

limitless realms

Of unexplored reality,

And together we'll say Yes!

To a Unified Field of energy

Grounded

In Love.

4.27.13

It's time

To slow way down,

Lower the volume,

Take a deep breath-

Mmmmmmmmm......

Gentle, quiet,

Listening with every cell

To the light vibrating

All around and

Through us.

Allowing the Mother

Earth herself to

So completely

Give us

Her full and natural

Effortless support-

So that we might let go

Of everything and just

Give ourselves to Her

In total trust and

Final surrender.

What a great act of courage

We could make by just

Laying down

And being still.

4.29.13

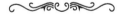

In any given moment,

Joy can arrive,

Un-announced

Un-contrived

Undeniably

True-

As the eye

Of a randomly-appearing

Dolphin

Suddenly smiles

Into mine,

And declares:

"Why worry?

Isn't it obvious?

Everything is perfectly

OK!"

Well then.

The universe has spoken

Today,

Loud and clear,

In no uncertain terms:

"Rest easy,

Be attentive,

And open to the miraculous

Now"

I'm listening...

5.1.13

When the world

Seems to threaten

Or hold you down,

Don't panic;

Don't despair-

Just let yourself relax

And know

That eventually,

You'll be released,

Float back to the surface,

And come up

For air.

It may seem like

Forever,

But really,

No time passed at all,

And now,

We can breathe

Deeply together,

And even sob

Huge tears

Of gratitude

And relief.

There are so many

Miracles

Around every corner

Of our existence-

If we could only

Trust enough

To open so wide

That our hearts, minds,

Souls and perceptions

Could actually be present

For the gifts

Of spiritual grace

That are always

Right here,

Ready

To be received.

5.2.13

Where can we find Love today-

If we look outside

Of our own loving hearts?

Inside that great

Chamber of Infinite Potential

Is an endless

Ocean of compassion,

Where Light dances

With every appearance,

And all beings who enter

Are cherished and welcomed

With so much tenderness

That all they can do is respond

With Love.

5.3.13

We choose

To take

The middle way-

Between light and shadow

And beyond the play

Of all the petty

Disturbances

In this world.

A magic lives

Just below

The surface of things,

Out of view

But for the few

Who long

So fervently

To see the root

And live the truth.

And here, at last,

We find

The deeper connection,

The simple perfection,

The ease, the flow

And the absolute joy

Of letting go.

5.4.13

What if

Each and every

Pore in our body

Were a portal

To another dimension?

And what

If every cell

Were a universe unto itself?

Would we breathe

Into those new dimensions;

Explore those endless

Universes,

And feel everything

That keeps us

From being

In total, ecstatic reunion

With the entire cosmos

Of our own

Miraculous being?

And then- to move, with so much

Awareness,

Tenderness,

And appreciation

For the absolute,

Unspeakable Miracle

That is life in this vehicle

Of love.

5.5.13

Just how subtle

Can we possibly be?

As subtle as the silent earth-

Holding us so patiently

In her ever-present Embrace...

As subtle as the spring rain-

Melting everything so gently

And washing it all

Back to the sea...

As subtle as this quiet breath-

So tenderly exploring

Every atom

Of the inner expanse

Of this human body...

As subtle as the secret spark

Of intuition that leaps

Ahead to light the flame

Of deep awareness...

Or as subtle

As the all-pervading life in space,

Existing without effort,

And connecting everything

To everything

And guiding us always

Back to Source...

Today, perhaps

We could just be...

So Subtle.

5.6.13

In what form

Would you like

To explore

The essence

Of your

True nature?

Are you a

Goddess Dancing

In the body of a man

Who sees

The Goddess

Dancing

Below the surface

Of everything?

What magic

Might you sing

When opening

Into realms

Beyond beauty

And pain?

What infinitesimal

Wink of an eyelash

Might set

A fabulous crusade

Of wildly rapturous

Hummingbirds

In motion to vibrate

The entire situation

Into new and unknown

Dimensions?

Or just this

Simple life,

Floating between

Water and air,

Trusting completely

That whatever the tides bring

Will be exactly

What's needed

For the next

Perfect

Adventure.

5.7.13

Did you ever feel

Like your soul

Might have pulled back a bit,

Folded in on itself,

Way back when,

For protection from

The pain and terror of

Devastating overwhelm?

Now I'm feeling

Everything all the way back to my DNA-

And I sense

That the Truth

Of this awareness

Actually encompasses

All time and space,

All dimensions,

All realities-

And holding gently

All those feelings

In this vast and eternal

Ocean of compassion-

We witness

Each wound and scar

Returning to its origin and

Releasing enough energy

To fuel a new universe

Forever.

And we might remember

That bright morning in Spring

When we danced

For the New Moon in May,

And garlanded

Our love

With wildflowers-

And the Earth Herself

Moved through our

Vibrating bodies,

In celebration

Of the rebirth

Of joy.

5.8.13

Turtle teaching today:

No matter what

Arises-

Just stay

Right here in the flow,

And Breathe as deeply

As needed to release everything

On the outbreath-

Because- after all-

Is there anything

That we can really

Hold onto anyway?

There's only one perception

That's absolutely clear-

And that's this dance

Of ever-changing light

That seems to be

The all-pervasive

Truth

Of this existence.

And,

When all is said and done-

What else are we

Than this:

The motion

Of the sweet sun's radiance

Through the crystal waters

Of our souls.

5.9.13

What kind of beauty will we find

When we follow our breath

To the secret places

Only it knows how to feel?

Such simplicity and depth

Of awareness,

Such an achingly

Vast

Open-ness

To experience-

This is the only path

My heart can See.

5.10.13

Amazing to experience

The wind-blown

Wild, chaotic existence

On the surface-

And then,

To dive just below-

And see

The peaceful, quiet,

Deep blue world,

So full of life-

An entire universe

Existing in harmony

With itself.

Back and forth,

Breathing between

Indivisible dimensions,

That support and penetrate

each other as lovers-

And just allowing

ourselves to move

Like a warm current

through cool water...

Accepting every sensation

As energy

That feeds awareness-

Until that moment comes,

Like magic,

And we find ourselves

In the heart

Of a wave,

Flying in joyous

Light and

Creativity,

Dancing

In love with

Everything.

5.11.13

In this body

I bow

To the Mother,

Who gave us all

Life~

And keeps us

Alive, still~

With every breath,

Every step on this

Green earth,

Every drop of water,

Every taste of nourishment,

Every sense perception~

Feeding us

Directly

From Her Womb

Of Compassion.

And let us now

Vow

To preserve and protect Her,

As She has preserved and protected us,

Through all the lifetimes

Of our expanding awareness-

From first emergence

As single-cell

Organisms,

Through the entire

Passionate journey

Of our evolving DNA,

We have been

So gently

Held

And nurtured,

Encouraged,

And loved.

From beginningless time

To endless eternity

I dedicate myself

To serve the Mother

Of us all.

5.12.13

Exertion

In exactly

The right increment

Of energy expenditure-

This leads to the bliss

Of a wild swim

Against the wind,

Wide open,

The whole world

Flowing through the center

Like stars falling

Through the galactic gateway-

And it feels like

The Universe

Is actually pulling the strength

Through this body

To meet itself-

And that

Feels like

Making love

To everything.

And then,

The joyous release

And spin,

Wheeling through the water,

Head-over-heels,

Picking up speed

Till momentum peaks

And we're flying home now

With the current,

Riding the ocean swell,

No thought, nor even

Any self at all-

Just this beautiful light

And energy

Moving with perfect grace

Through time and space

In complete

Equanimity.

5.13.13

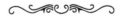

There's a light

Inside,

Shining so bright

We might

Be scared to look-

But if we do,

We'll see beyond

The casual chaos

Of daily encounters

With a world

Out-of-balance...

We'll see the brilliance

That we were born with,

Unfettered,

Undefiled,

Unmarked

By the trials and rigors

Of life in human society...

And if we let that light

Shine out through our eyes,

From our hearts and

From every particle

Of our being-

It will guide us

So gently,

So easily

And effortlessly

Through all the mazes

Of our days,

And everywhere we go~

Everywhere we look~

We will see that light

Reflected

In other eyes

And flowers

And brightly shining

Down from the sky,

Singing to our souls

The lovesong

That we learned

Before time began.

5.14.13

Sometimes Life requires of us

The precision of a pointillist painter,

Or the patience and detachment

Of a Tibetan sand artist...

And all we need to do

Is pay attention to each point,

Each grain of sand,

As if that's all there is

In the whole universe,

And that nano-second

Contains the concentrated

Essence of all eternity.

As we enter the trance

Of Full Presence to this Now,

Everything inessential

Is completely stripped away:

We are cleansed

Down to the molecular level,

And the eye of the needle

Becomes no problem

To negotiate.

Take my hand,

We can step through

Together,

And enter the realm

Of Heaven

On Earth.

5.15.13

Staying Present

Through the trials,

Tragedies and traumas

That arise and pass-

Feeling everything to the core,

With curiosity,

As though it were

An intensely interesting adventure-

We can heal

For ourselves

And for others-

All the concepts held

For so long

About suffering and shame,

Badness and blame-

Why not

Make it all

Into the most beautiful

Song-

And see

Just how much deeper

The music can really get...

Yes, dive down

Down, below the melody,

Below the chord,

Below the rhythm-

To the light

Pulsing in the heartbeat,

Moving through the blood and bones,

Sparking from the fingertips,

Weaving through the night-

A tapestry of love

And magic

That wraps us all

So tenderly

In the warmest embrace

Of the Divine Mother's

Unconditional Compassion.

5.16.13

Do you wonder

Just how

It's even possible

To do everything

That we do?

From the little daily tasks

To the big events of a lifetime-

It's all actually

Quite miraculous.

Today,

While bodysurfing 10-foot waves,

Pulling drowning humans in to shore,

And chanting the Quan Yin

Goddess of Compassion Mantra

to myself, I thought:

It's really impossible,

If we try to do it

All ourselves.

And if we just

Completely surrender

And let the

Ever-present Energy

Of the Universe

Move through us,

As it wants to-

Responding precisely

And appropriately

To whatever situation

happens to arise-

Then- Voila!

We have super-powers,

Because, hey- don't you know-

The Universe

And the Goddess of Compassion

Are actually limitless Sources

Of exactly what's needed

For any given moment.

So here we are-

In the Heart

Of a Galactic Storm,

And all we need to do

Is breathe.

5.17.13

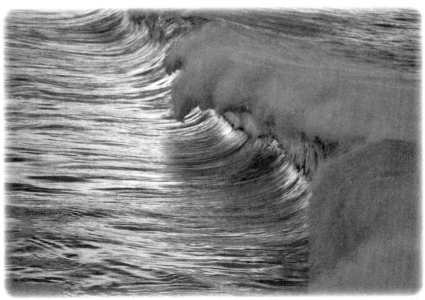

Photo Credit: Leilani Zerkle

Please take my hand:

It's time to

Dive off the cliff

At the end of forever,

And see what

Awaits us there...

This morning we open

To the light

And embrace the dark

And feel all the way into

Infinity~

With the emerging awareness

Of this Planetary Being

Who walks and talks

And thinks and feels

Through us and our bodies~

And if we really feel

Everything that She is feeling-

Here we are-

All together,

Spinning around the golden sun,

In absolute love and terror,

Hurtling through space

In a geometrically vast musical rhapsody

Humans call

"The Solar System"

That's just a small part

Of this galaxy

We call

"The Milky Way"

That's just a small part of this

Universe,

That's just one

Of infinite possible universes...

And today,

We ride warm waves of bliss,

Bathed in gold and blue

Clear crystal waters,

Flying together

Across the bay

Of our sweet dreamworld-

And is there anything more important than this?

Sharing our presence,

And sending the goodness

Of each moment of wonder

Out to touch everyone

And everything

With the radiant glow

Of true, brilliant,

Joy.

5.18.13

Let's just stay right here

For a while,

And see

What it feels like

Not

To go anywhere,

Or do anything

Or try,

Or even think-

Let's just stop

Everything,

And see what happens...

Maybe,

The Universe Herself

Will finally

Feel welcome

To enter in

To our cells,

Exploring the spirals

Of our DNA,

And even

The convolutions

Of our multitudinous,

Multifaceted

Minds.

And if She

Really feels

Our full permission,

She might even

Enter our hearts,

And fill us

So Full

Of the Love

That She has always felt,

Till we overflow,

At last becoming

Our natural selves:

The True Expressions

Of Her Essence

Moving through bodies

On Planet Earth.

5.20.13

Love knows no limits,

Nor concepts,

Or even the beginnings

Of boundaries.

The smile of a child

Cuts through all resistance,

And pulls the heart

Straight out, into full

Present

Awareness.

And with that attention we walk

Gently through the world,

Observing

The deep crystal blue waters of life

That surround us,

And tuning in

To the most refined

Vibrations of joy,

The tiniest buzz of a bee

Or the softest touch

Of a baby's cheek-

Every detail of the day

A doorway

Into the unborn,

Immortal realm

Of love.

5.21.13

Random encounters

Grant us the gift, of an opportunity

To share our love

With the universe.

No matter what arises, we can choose-

To listen; to breathe, and pay attention

To the details of the situation...

Maybe, someone needs help-

They might be drowning,

In the undertow of a big swell-

And our timing is of the essence-

Get to them,

Give them support and calm,

And use exactly the energy necessary

To bring them safely to shore.

Or a small child

In a strange place might need

A gentle smile

And a sweet song

To brighten her afternoon,

And bring her beautiful grandfather

Happiness.

All we need to do is show up

And be appropriate-

Exactly like

Finding the perfect Harmony

For whatever music is happening.

And that's all

There is

To it.

5.22.13

There's a quiet place

That we remember

Before memory-

A silent space,

Dark like

A velvet night

With a million

Godzillion

Stars

Sparkling

With some kind

Of indescribably blue

Light,

That caresses our souls

In a way so tender

And complete,

We can only

Imagine

It must be

Exactly like

The warmth

Of the womb.

And so,

Let us accept

The intrinsic invitation

Of that un-knowable,

Immeasurable

Expanse,

And allow ourselves

The greatest gift

Of absolute

Surrender-

Just give it all,

Every last particle,

Every thought,

Every word

Every sensation, emotion, perception,

The whole entire

Package-

Let's please

Just drop it all

Right over the edge

Into emptiness,

And follow it,

Falling

Forever

Into the truth

Of complete awareness,

And the ultimate

Rebirth

Of our own,

Magical Essence.

5.23.13

So curious to discover

What world of wonder

Will emerge

From this

Tiny

Yellow drop

Of bright sunshine.

Like a seed

Holding all the

Hidden potential

Of a great tropical

Fruit tree in full bloom,

Each moment

Carries the possibility

Of such great generosity,

That were we

To stop completely,

And pay attention,

We might find ourselves

At such a feast,

We could never have imagined,

Nor toiled to create.

Wonderment

Implies emptiness~

And this subtle appetite

For knowing reality

Exactly as it is,

Makes of each breath

The greatest gift,

Without the slightest

Idea or assumption about

What the next one

Might bring.

Such gratitude and grace!

So dance with me now,

And we will all

Dance together,

And when the perfect time comes,

We will Sing.

5.24.13

The ability to feel

The non-duality

Of our own True nature

Allows us the space

To really be inside each other.

Looking out

Of your eyes,

I see colors

I'd never imagined,

And sensing the world

Through your skin,

I experience

The universe

In a whole new dimension.

Our souls

Spiral around

And through each other,

Deepening wisdom,

Opening understanding,

And expanding

The capacity

For love.

There's not a breath

Without your presence,

Nor yet a single step

Without your hand in mine.

This isn't some kind

Of dependence

Or helpless merging...

This isn't a defense

Against the truth,

But a surrender to it-

The undeniable

Fact

That we are one being

Manifesting through two souls,

Exploring the planet

In separate bodies,

And united forever

In the simple acceptance

Of our

Undivided Perfection.

5.25.13

In a vast open space

A million multicolored lights

Emerge, and fill this body

Until every cell is vibrating,

Every nerve ending

Humming,

And the light dances and sings,

Taking the shape

Of this vessel

Of skin and sinew,

Radiating out

Through every pore,

And connecting

With every awakened being

To fulfill the ancient promise

And return the homeland

To harmony.

5.26.13

Find the root

In the core of the planet;

Feel the firmness of a mountain,

And the flexibility

Of a river

Flowing down

To the sea...

There's a waterfall

Of crystalline light

Pouring through our

Open central channel,

And a Goddess

Guiding us

With grace-

We can float

Or fly,

Sit in silence

Or walk in wonderment

As each step

Unfolds like a fairytale

Of magic and beauty.

There's no doubt

That this journey

Is grounded in the truth–

We have felt the wounds of millennia

And faced the fears of ancestral grief–

Yet now:

An opening,

A portal,

An ascension–

Leaving no essence behind,

We gather the delicate pollen of our souls' reality

And attend to the task of making honey.

5.27.13

When we fully explore

A form

With good attention-

Whether it takes

The shape

Of our own body,

Or a flower,

Or a daily ritual-

Or a piece of music,

Or a thought

Or even

A feeling

Like rage or terror-

When we give

Ourselves completely

And just let ourselves

Be with whatever

Is currently present-

Then

The miracle,

The magic,

The marvelous can emerge...

All the excess

And extravagance

And extraneous

Trappings of ego

Just fall away

And dissolve

In the clarity of vision,

The care and precision

With which we attend

The current situation-

And all that remains

Is this beauty and grace,

This subtle romance

With reality,

This empathic

Dance

With the power

Of true existence.

5.28.13

There's a music

Singing through me

Like a bubbling

River of light-

Any time,

Anywhere-

I just listen,

And it's there...

Flowing through

This heart and body,

Emptying out the mind of excess,

Filling up the soul

With beauty-

Leading my entire being

Back to true

Communion.

Such gratitude

And grace I feel

For this song

That's been my guide forever-

Such an overwhelming willingness

To dedicate my life to this-

And such a full

And everlasting faith

That this path

Has chosen me,

And will care for me

And take me

All the way

Home.

5.29.13

Do you feel

How we are all

Just parts of Love

Falling in love

With itself?

Swimming

Through the waters

Of the world,

Sensing our

Cellular connectivity

With every living creature-

The light dances

Through each of us

And whispers

A song of longing

For reunion.

At some point,

The old patterns of clinging and rejection

Just disappear-

Suddenly,

The whole charade

Has faded into mist,

And what remains

Is this precious

Blue pearl of beauty.

Come now, Great Mother:

Move through me

Into all the realms of existence;

And return all beings

To your

Compassionate

Embrace.

5.30.13

Moving

Into the next

Time-space continuum

Vortex-

And remaining

Still,

In this body,

Breathing,

Effortless,

Aware.

There's a cave

Somewhere

In the Himalayas

For which

My soul

Sometimes longs-

And yet,

My work is in the world-

While never of it...

So each day

Begins with silence,

And ends the same way-

And in between,

I carry that silence with me

Like a talisman...

And from that

Sweet, velvet void,

The inner eye

Shines brightly,

And the inner ear

Knows the true harmony,

And every sense is attuned

To the one light of love

Emerging always from the heart.

We are willing,

Now, to learn this dance together,

And as our lights

Weave around each other

In a glowing net of gold,

We surround the globe

With the wonder of a realm

Beyond old paradigms,

United by shared vision,

And growing daily

To be

The manifested reality

Of our oldest,

Truest

Dreams.

5.31.13

So interesting

To discover

The journey we made-

How it began

In the womb

Of darkness and warmth-

How impressions

Of fear

Were laid

On that

Sensitive soul,

And the body

In its very formation

Took the posture

Of pain...

Return with me now

To the place

Before wounding,

And let us unwind

The whole story,

Till we find

That nothing

Is holding us

From being

Our wholeness,

And all of our

Multifaceted

Crystalline

Awareness

Is clear,

Present

And vibrantly

Alive.

6.1.13

When every breath

Is a journey

Of pleasure

And joy,

And our bodies

A wonder

Of beauty

To explore-

Then

All the stress

And tension

Of lifetimes

On red-alert

Are gone,

And we can rest

In realizing

That all this inquiry,

This practice

Of searching

For the roots

Of suffering

And holding them

Till they heal...

This hasn't been

Just personal at all-

It's been

For all of our

Ancestors, our DNA,

And for the Planet

Herself...

And as this knowing

Deepens in our souls,

We're given the strength,

Wisdom,

Courage and clarity

To continue

Till every particle,

Every being,

Every

Last

One

Can come home

Together.

6.2.13

Cherish the light

And beauty

Of love

In a world

Gone mad

With cruelty

And confusion...

Breathe

With your brothers

And sisters,

And stand strong

Together

In the vision

Of a planet

Returned to harmony.

The dying rage

Of a patriarchal

Age of insanity

Is the last despair of a doomed, demented

Race of Demons...

Our task is clear:

Remain rooted

In earth's reality,

With wisdom and restraint-

Nurture ourselves

And each other,

While cleansing everything

Within and without,

Down to the nano-particle,

And out to the most distant star...

Be willing and true,

Feel every feeling,

Deny nothing-

Cut through the veils,

Open every aperture

All the way

Till every photon of available

Luminosity

Feels completely welcome

To fill the void

And return like a pod

Of a million laughing dolphins

To the joyous being

Of Original Essence.

6.3.13

Let me be

A crystal vase

Of clear pure water,

To receive the flowers

Left by the beloved.

I no longer know

Who or what

That may be-

But have no doubt

That She

Is Ever-Present.

And so,

Breathing in

The foamy white light

Of a thousand galactic star-births,

I leave behind

All narcissistic notions,

And let Her Noble Presence

Rule my every expression.

She might manifest

In a million myriad forms-

And I would dance with each,

Without distinction,

Understanding that my one true love

Is here always,

And that we are but one universe

Making love to itself-

In a flow of

Interestingly individuated Awareness...

Exploring

Every dimension,

To know ourselves

Completely.

6.5.13

Photo Credit: Desiree' K. DallaGuardia

This mind seems to have lost

The distinctions

Between left and right-

And yet there remains

A space

In which the Ultimate

May unfold.

Today a wave

May take us

Way beyond the known-

And we might find ourselves

Deep in the Blue zone

Of the Great Mother's

Sweetest

Pleasure dome-

And here,

There's nothing to do

But be

Completely involved,

With every cell,

Every spiraling part

Of our selves

Present

And awake

To the rapture

Of oneness.

6.4.13

When the mind

Finally

Comes unglued

From its inherent

Self-absorption-

Suddenly everything

Becomes so

Fascinatingly undetermined...

Playing music for a crowd

And seeing each person

As an ephemeral

Wave-form-

Oscillating between

Dimensions of light

And sound...

Feeling waterfalls of emotion

Pour through this body

Like spiraling flows of love

Between Earth and Sky...

No language,

No interference,

No attempts at analysis,

Nor any attachment to space

Or time...

Just this passionate song

And the longing

For its essence.

Just this

Bubbling wellspring of beauty

And the devotion to its perfection.

Just this

Ongoing exploration

Of existence

Beyond the veils of illusion.

Choosing to die

Each moment

With an open heart,

To allow the world of dreams

A doorway

Into reality-

Each breath

Becomes a window

Into immortality.

6.6.13

In darkness or light,

It doesn't matter,

I'm here,

Feeling you

All through the night-

In rapture

Or in despair,

The soul remains the same-

We touch deeper than skin,

Embracing across oceans

And time

No longer has dominion.

Listen, for a moment

With me

To the velvet silence

Of our heart's desire-

And the song that emerges

Is the lantern that leads us,

Dancing,

Into the realm of Light Beams

And flower ornaments-

Where one crystal teardrop

Contains oceans of compassion,

And all of our

Sweetest dreams

Are true.

6.7.13

At the end of forever

Is a wild, open space

Where dragons live

Free and dangerous-

Unknown

Uninhibited

Unthinkably

Huge.

Today,

Let's go there

And ride out into

The vast uncharted territories

Too terrifyingly

Delicious

To even imagine

Before.

We'll explore

Every multi-dimensional

Possibility

Of total

Tantric exuberance.

Not even the tiniest

Nor greatest desire

Will go unsatisfied-

They will all run,

Screaming with glee

Into the great singularity

At the Heart of Everything-

And dissolve

In our passion

For the truth.

Then, stark-soul-naked

In the brilliant luminosity

Of the benevolent gaze

Of the Goddess,

We will merge

Again,

You, and I

and the cosmos,

Reunited

In the ultimate bliss

Of absolute

Openness.

6.8.13

Being in a body,

Breathing-

Feeling every

Sense scintillating

With the sparkle

Of vibrant life.

The great magnetic waves of love

From this planet's living core

Move up through our toes

And out through our fingertips,

To touch everything

With the blessings

Of tender awareness.

Each and every

Multidimensional aspect

Of this quotidian quixotic adventure

Is a reflection to move us deeper

In-

To appreciation

Of the miracle

That is our own

Manifestation,

As sentient creatures

Who are learning

How to share

And care for each other.

Don't doubt

Even one sacred breath...

Just breathe it and know

That the next will come

In its own natural

Perfection.

6.8.13

Sometimes it seems

That our souls

Need some

Resistance

To grow,

Like a green shoot

Coming up through the earth

In Spring.

Sometimes we just

Have to swim

Against the flow,

To make ourselves

Strong

And let our bodies

Thrive and sing.

It's not

That any effort

At all is required-

Just breathing

With the situation

And allowing

The natural

Response to arise.

And then-

Like alchemical

Magic in a bottle,

Our spirits

Start to foam

And froth

With the joy

Of being precisely

Present

To whatever is real.

And within this

Crucible of awareness,

The impurities

Are boiled away,

And the sweet

Elixir

Of pure essential

Beauty

Is poured out-

To return

Like a river

To the sea.

6.9.13

Everywhere

We dream

Of angels

And demons-

And nothing

Can really

Take us to the truth,

But this

Single breath,

That returns,

To swallow us

Whole

Into the depths

Of our own

Unimpeded

Perception.

I'm not going

Anywhere anymore-

No, please-

Just hang me

Upside down

From this great world

Tree,

Until all the spare change

Just falls

Out of my pockets,

And I'm left,

Well and finally

Empty

Of everything.

No hurry,

Just hangin'

Here forever,

Offered up as a gift

To the Goddess

Who once knew me

Before the womb.

And then,

When we've come

All the way through,

And left

Even the forest behind-

We'll stand together

Gazing out at forever...

In a moment,

We'll feel a warm updraft-

And trusting our wings,

We'll fly.

6.11.13

We've chanted

The name of the Goddess

One hundred and eight times,

And fasted for fourteen days,

And taken vows of silence,

Abstinence and worse...

But maybe

All that's needed

Is a day with the trees,

Listening to the whisper

Of the breeze

Kissing the leaves

And bathing

In the green glow of nature's

Effortless Compassion.

She doesn't ask

For any return–

Just offers her

Sweet waters freely-

And in the warm tenderness

Of her embrace,

We are entirely absolved

Of past and future

Peccadillos,

Returned to zero,

And given

Freedom to be

Reconnected

With everything.

For a while, let's simply

Sit

In this realm

Of simple miracles,

And breathe.

6.12.13

Photo Credit: Morris Henry Lax

Do you remember

The time

You tried, as a child,

Some new adventure-

Like walking,

Or talking to a tree

Or maybe

Your first time

Ever

On a roller skate?

There was this deep

And absolute

Trust-

Combined with enthusiastic confidence,

And no thought whatsoever

Of failure-

Just this avid curiosity

Concentrating

On every beautiful detail

Of the fully embodied

Present moment.

And in this current incarnation,

We've opened again

The wild world

Of wonder~

Where nothing

Is pre-ordained,

And everything

Holds the magic

Of infinite

Possibility.

Closing our eyes,

We reach out

In any given direction,

And touch someone

Who is sharing

The same dream.

And as we sense the contact,

All of us

Come awake

Together, and laughing,

Singing, skipping and spinning,

We're ready

For the next miraculous moment.

6/13/13

Somehow, it seems

That this struggle

Does not

Belong to me.

So for now, I think I'll wait,

And watch,

And just keep

Breathing in

The understanding-

That there's a balance

In all things,

And a natural geometry

Whose spiraling symmetry

Is fueled by chaos,

Bounded by emptiness,

And is continually aware

In the spontaneous creation

Of music and light.

Just keeping still,

Listening attentively,

Gives this Great Magic

The space to work its wonders...

And if we let go so completely

That all notions of duality

Disappear...

Then the sweet spring

Will rise from the desert floor,

Filling the arid expanse

With life-giving water,

And confounding

The forces of the pharaoh,

While we walk,

Unimpeded,

Into the Promised Land.

6.13.13

Each day

Is calling us

To take another

Great leap

Into the unknown.

Whether absorbing the silence,

Stillness

And wisdom

Of the nearest

Inanimate

Object;

Or swimming full-strength

Through dark and murky water

And emerging suddenly

Into a liquid blue cathedral

Full of dancing color and light...

The inner experience

Remains

Raw,

Naked

And achingly filled

With nothing

But awe.

Even the very next breath

Is as distant

And mysterious

As a galaxy

A million light-years

From now.

Just this

Present sensation

Of tingling awareness

In every vibrating cell,

All the way

Down to the DNA

That's singing its secret song

Of love and longing

To the universe Herself...

Just this

Foaming, fizzing,

Unfathomable unfolding

Of life-force

Flowing through us

And out

Into the great

Eternal wonderfulness

Of this

Existence.

6/14/13

A single tone

Sounds in the night,

And reality shifts,

To embrace this

New frequency-

Bringing our body

Into resonance,

And allowing our souls

To harmonize.

Thus, with even

The most subtle

Of brainwaves

Or emanations of

The Heart,

We can dance

In the realms of light

And magic,

And, with love

Bring more beauty

Into this thirsty world.

So we sit quietly,

Listening-

For that one song

That will lead us

Again

Back to the core

From which

Music

Is born.

6.15.13

In this life,

And most of my previous ones,

I was never much into

The "Father-God" thing.

For me dakine was the Goddess...

Protect Her, Serve Her,

Love Her in All

Her aspects...

I've always felt that,

Until True Balance is returned

To the human socio-political and sexual situation,

Women and the Goddess

Deserve obvious priority.

And now we're in a shift-

Still lagging way behind true

Equanimity-

Yet it seems that we men

As well as women,

Need to really learn

To give each other, and ourselves

Some true Respect...

As in honoring

Our own divinity,

Male and female alike...

Which brings us back

To the question of God...

Perhaps this

Whole gender thing,

This whole

Dualistic approach,

Is just a huge

Diversion

From the truth.

Perhaps,

We're all just humans,

Gods and goddesses,

Plants and fish and wild animals-

Rocks and trees

And butterflies,

Sharing this outrageously,

Overwhelmingly beautiful

Little planet

In a spectacular solar system

That's flying through a galaxy

In a universe of wonders.

Maybe we could all

Just learn

To care for each other,

With tenderness.

6.16.13

Souls know

Each other instantly-

Without the need

For introductions

Or even a moment

Of small talk.

Our communication

Is pure

And our trust

Is complete.

Like a Mozart duet

We dance,

And the natural romance

That emerges from our music

Is like the sweet-smelling blossoms

Of joy

On a cherry tree in the Spring.

Don't doubt

That distance disappears

In the moonlight

Of our magic.

Come lay with me here

In this hidden

Garden of the Heart,

And we will explore

All the intricacies

Of our two

Intertwining universes

That have now become

One.

6.17.13

When the trade winds

Come charging

Like a cavalcade

Of wild Mongol horsemen

Out of the North,

The waves rise up

In excitement

And anticipation,

And we water-beings,

With rapt attention,

Await the perfect

Wedge...

This takes patience

And precision,

And being completely present

To current reality...

And then-

When all the conditions come together,

We pump our bodies

Into the surf,

And fly down the face of the wave,

Every line of our form

In continuous contact,

As though we were making love

With the entire ocean

Along that single ride-

Gliding, spiraling and giddy

With the joy

Of transcendent union.

Each moment,

Each detail

Of this unfolding life

Is asking for the same

Joy, enthusiasm, and devotion...

There can be

No discrimination,

Nor judgment,

No preference,

Nor pushing away...

It's all one

Reality,

And each wave

Requires the same

Absolute

Love.

6.19.13

Can you

Meet me here

In the warm summer

Moonlit night-

And we

Will let our souls

Turn to silver

As our naked hearts unfold...

There's no reason

For hesitation-

Just allow

The old robes

And all the other seasons

To fall away-

We can dance and pray

To the sky

And the sea,

Breathing in

The waves of love from the Earth

Through our toes,

And breathing out

We give it all up

To the stars.

Yes, do

Join our bodies

In one song

That reaches

From eternity to infinity–

Expressing every dimension of being

And leading us at last

Into the golden

Dawn.

6.21.13

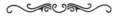

The wind sings

Through the chimes

Outside my window, a song

Of longing and release,

Of emptiness and opening...

And if we could allow

Our hearts to gently follow

That meandering melody-

It would lead us outward

To a shimmering silver pathway

Across the sea,

And up, into the sky-

Right through the great huge

Glowing moon,

And beyond–

Till we find ourselves

Waltzing

With the stars–

So sweetly serenaded

By the deep

Soft velvet night,

That we cannot help

But dance all the way

Into the arms

Of bliss.

6.22.13

Sing praise

To the Goddess of Compassion,

And trust

In the benevolent nature

Of the ultimate dimension.

Here is a great gift—

A day begun

In quiet contemplation,

Cleansing and nourishing

Body and soul.

Continued in joyful exertion,

Riding waves of beauty

Through the Great Waters

Of life.

As the sun sets, and the full moon rises,

We turn to the horizon,

And drink in the golden rays—

Bathing every cell

In sacred patterns of light,

And receiving the wisdom-stream

Straight from the heart

Of Reality.

Cherishing this gift

With care and gratitude,

We turn again to the world,

And share all the colors of music

To heal every soul

And bring the sweetness

Of this day

Into flowering

Fulfillment.

6.23.13

When standing on the precipice

Of the infinite unknown,

One always has the choice-

To feel terror

Or exhilaration,

Or just

To fall backwards

Into emptiness-

And breathe-

The endless possibilities

Rising up,

Passing through us-

And we remain here,

Weightless

Beyond all resistance,

And lightyears

From any handhold

On previously known realities...

Such great joy,

Passion and power arise

From this simple embrace

Of the truth of

Our condition.

Naked to the Universe,

We dance-

And She,

Seeing our receptivity,

Strums the strings of our souls,

And we sing.

6.25.13

Noting how

Excruciatingly real

Everything is right now,

And how

Completely vaporous

And dreamlike

At the very same time.

Paying exquisite attention

To the most minute

Particles of perfection

In my periphery-

And still feeling

Our complete connection

With the boundless black void

Of empty space that hums

Gently

Between galaxies.

When we sink

Into the dark core

Of our belly-root,

And drink

The sweet nectar

Of Mother-Earth's

Magnetic juices...

Then all the differences

Between devils and deities

Disappear,

And we are left whole,

Untroubled

And at peace

With the entirety

Of creation.

6.26.13

Golden glow

Fills the air

As the day gives itself up

To evening–

And the world becomes quiet

For a moment,

As if in prayer...

The birds are left

With their songs to the sky,

And we listen,

Allowing music

To emerge

For the night.

Look, there's light

Emanating from our fingertips,

As they dance across

Silver strings–

And Wood resonates against skin

As we sense the magic within.

An alchemy so ancient

We can access its imprint

On our souls, in our spiraling DNA-

The vessel of the heart

Opens to receive

The intertwining energies

Of our Mother Planet

And of the Universe through which

She flies...

We feel Her within us

Loving, and Beloved-

Creating root rhythms

In the blood,

Calling rhapsodies

Forth from the bones,

And harmonies from every part

Of our enraptured being.

Every sensation is surrendered

To this one breath of creation-

Every amount

Of attention is given completely

To this one melody...

And in the great work of merging

All present energies

Into one symphonic union,

We are refined and transfigured,

Leaving only

The sublime nectar

Of our own

Sweet essence.

6.27.13

Amazing

How anything can happen,

Any time-

And we just

Attend to the situation-

Glassy waves?

We ride them-

Sunshine and beauty?

Breathe it all in-

Wild winds and huge swell?

Dance with everything

That arises,

Loving it,

Feeling it,

Being with it

All the way through.

There's such a wonderfully

Deliciously subtle

Sizzling hum running through this body-

Like eighty-six million

Flickering beams of light

Exploring all the activity

Within and without,

And channeling

All those photonic particles of love

Into one central swirl

That runs up the line

From sacred sacrum

To holy crown-

And makes all this

Exciting existence

Such a pleasurable

Possibility.

6.28.13

When the day

Has been so full

Of every feeling,

And all your energy

Has pumped through you

Beyond your known capacity-

And hey, guess what,

It's required to

Rock the house right now,

One more time, again...

Well then-

Only one solution-

Just get

Completely

Out of the way

And let the music

Be.

Because, you know,

We've trained for this-

Our bodies are fine-tuned

Receptors,

And all we need

Is to listen so wide

Open to the sound

That's waiting, so ready-

So huge and endless and beyond all beauty-

Wrapped around our skin

And emerging

From within...

We're silent,

Gone to the other shore,

And the great wave

Of tender power and compassion

From the Moon's constant tide

Rides through us,

Carrying the rapture

And the rhapsody,

The melody

And harmony-

All combined to bring

Another song into being-

And all that's left to do

Is play.

6/29/13

This day

I am choosing to let go

Of yesterday and of tomorrow–

And also

Of joy and of sorrow–

Of you and I,

And even of high and of low–

Thoughts and feelings,

And all the words and ideas

That make up these poems–

They too, can go–

For now

It's time

To finally close the door

On ego,

And open the window

Of the soul.

6.30.13

Stillness;

Like a mountain lake

At sunrise-

Calm and serene

And ready

To reflect the light

And color

Of the coming day.

Quiet-

Like the deep

Pre-dawn star-filled void,

That knows

Only the wild emptiness

Of infinite expanse.

These qualities

Are so exquisitely subtle

Yet so powerful

That they capture

Our souls,

And hang them like Christmas lights

Across our corner

Of the cosmos–

And then what's left to do,

But sparkle,

And shine.

7.1.13

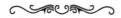

Between dream and dreamer,

Real and surreal,

Feelings and the one

Who feels them-

Are there any

True

Distinguishing factors?

It seems to this soul

That the delineations

Have begun to blur,

And that

Differing points of view,

Far from creating

More differences-

Simply make

A bigger picture

For all involved.

So now...

We spread the wide wings

Of our beautifully

Opening hearts,

And let every feather

Touch the tip

Of every other

Till all of us

Are fluttering so gently

Together-

And as one

Outrageously

Awakened being-

Let us all

Please

Rise.

7.2.13

Falling off the edge

Of everything

And floating

In the emptiness

Of true awareness...

Return now

To the water,

Return again

To the wave,

And be liquid,

Be blue,

Be brave enough

To go all the way through

To the other side;

The shoreless shore

Is calling.

The setting sun

Fills this vessel

With such a sweetness

That all other nourishment

Seems less

Than necessary.

Witnessing

The endless noise

Of minds out of balance

And spirits in distress,

You choose to go

Out in

To the dark and quiet night

And hold holy

Communion

With the silence

Of the stars.

A million million tiny points of light,

And we can rest

In the comfort

Of feeling our deepest connection

With every single

One.

7.3.13

Photo Credit: Don V Lax

We now declare

Our total freedom

From every form

Of inner or outer

Oppression:

Our ultimate

Independence from all

Attachment

To consumption,

And our interdependent,

Cooperative

Empowerment

To create a world

Rooted in compassion.

We now invoke

And dream awake

The full acceptance

Of every feeling,

Every color and vibration,

Without exception–

Including all facets

Of the great expanding crystal

Of this one true reality.

With joy and delight

We turn again

To come around right,

Hand-in hand

In the sweet spiral

That has been

Singing through our centers

Since our souls

First emerged

From bliss.

7.4.13

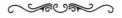

On this day,

Let us love

What we see,

And be

What we love.

Breathing in from our hearts

And out again

To infinity.

Completely grounded

In this awareness,

And completely open

To the multiverse of existence.

A birdsong,

A butterfly;

The ocean,

The sky...

The scent of flowers,

The taste of tragedy-

All merging

In one pure song

Of passionate

Experience.

Last night

A small girl

Danced in ecstatic abandon

To the sound of my violin,

Spinning through space and time

With her hands in the air-

And broke my heart

Wide open

Again.

7.6.13

In the darkest dark

Of the darkest night

Is a doorway

Into dimensions

Beyond our sight.

Come now, and swim

And we will flow

Right through that door

On a clear sweet stream

Of breath...

And here we find

Our root and crown

Connecting to the heart

Of everything:

The inner light

Shines bright

And shows the way

To sense

A universe of wonders.

How in the world

Can words describe

The essence of unspeakable

Magic?

Let's close our eyes

And open our souls

With all their senses and desires,

And feel our journey

Like passionate witnesses

To the truth

Of beauty.

7.7.13

The moon is New

And the day

And the sunshine too,

And each breath

A miracle

Of newness-

And everything sparkles

With an inner light

That we've never seen

Quite this way

Before.

This seemingly

Endless wave

Of bliss

That I'm riding

Is pouring

Through my center

And connecting

Inner to outer,

Earth and sea

To stars and sky

And all

The pain and ecstasy

Of a life

Lived full-strength,

Raw

And without

Any filters

Whatsoever.

Who needs honey

When you can have

Sweetness

Like that?

7.8.13

When we bow

To the sun as She sets,

Such a great

Gratitude

Sweeps through our souls!

Our minds and

Our bodies can open

Completely, and receive

Sweet blessings

From above.

A million messages of light

Dance through our DNA

And teach us

New language

And give us sight

To share new beauty.

Tonight

A thousand peacocks

Fan their plumage in my heart,

And give birth

To a song

So poignant

That tears tremble

From these eyes

As I witness

The music emerge.

Children dance,

Enraptured

By the refracted love

Only they can hear,

And we share

A secret,

And smile.

7.9.13

This precious moment

Is the one

That opens all the windows

Into light.

We've been standing

At the threshold

For a million years,

And now,

Why wait any longer?

Like a seabird

Plummeting from the sky

To find its fish,

We drop

Right off the edge

And fall

Into infinite wonder,

Where every wish

Was granted

Before it was even

Imagined.

And when, at last,

We reach the sea,

And rest-

The crystal blue loveliness

Surrounds and permeates us,

And all the energy

Of all the galaxies

(Humming as they spin),

Pours through our cores

And unites us

In the passionate embrace

Of deepest

Reality.

7.10.13

Subtle and effortless,

Breathing broad bands

Of light

Into every cell,

Every strand

Of DNA

Glows with effervescent

Fervor,

And we experience

Our bodies

As unified

Vibratory

Energy

That just loves

To dance.

This isn't some

Pipe dream

Or fantasy-

It's true Reality-

When the baggage

Is finally

Left behind,

And the ascending Planet

Given full permission

To move up

Through our bones

And infuse our hearts,

Minds and souls

With the Great Love

For the Universe

That's been there

All along.

7.11.13

When working with

The chaotic energy

That arises spontaneously

From life

In this universe-

The only path seems to be

Behind thoughts and feelings,

Forms and ideas-

Even further back

Than spirit-

In the secret center,

In the hidden chamber,

In the dimension beyond dimensions,

Where sun and moon

Are in constant

Passionate

Union...

This place leads us

Completely

Away from all known frequencies,

Into the unrecognizable spectrum

Of raw experience.

Just this

One breath:

Just this

Big Wave,

And no choice whatsoever

But to ride it

All the way

Home.

7.12.13

From heart to hands

And hands to heart

Is a spiral pathway

That sends and receives

Breath-like messages

Of energy

And love.

Fingers dancing

On silver strings

Are romancing

The secret flame

That dwells within

Every soul that ever lived

In this wonder-filled

Creation.

That's the only fire we wish to tend

Anymore at all–

No more

False hopes or distractions–

No more

Fantasies or fictions–

No more cool façade

Or masquerade...

Let's all vow,

From now on,

Never to settle

For anything less

Than the pure, raw

Hot and undiluted

Molten red lava

Sweet true nectar

Of the Goddess.

7.13.13

Let's give ourselves

Completely

To this.

Present and breathing

Awareness into every cell,

Vibrating full of dancing light

That merges in the heart

And emerges

As music.

When we're in that state,

Nothing else exists,

But the feeling

Of overwhelming love

And gratitude,

Tenderness with

Tears of compassion

For the lifetimes

Of separation from source

That we have all suffered.

And then even that

Dissolves

As the melody resolves

And we've gone beyond,

To the other shore

Where all

Is harmony.

7/14/13

The Goddess Gives us

This day

A lesson in being present

To the Wave.

Let the waves within

Be one with the waves you see...

Every oscillation

In every atom

Of every cell,

Loving

The waviness

Of wakefulness.

Watch now,

Listen, and feel

Deeply the sensations,

So subtle-

The warmth of the water

Might suddenly cool,

Or the reflection of light

May shift an inch or two

To the right

Or left-

And for sure

Never expect

A wave to appear

In the same size or shape

Or place-

Because

Isn't it true

That the very nature

Of waveforms

Is changeability?

As we breathe

And become

So gentle,

So receptive,

So absolutely open,

Quiet and ready-

Such a joy appears in our hearts

That everything external

Falls away

And we find ourselves

Riding that big, warm, glassy wave

In a state of blissful

Emptiness.

7.15.13

Gratitude

For everything

Sometimes arises

Like a wash of gentle tears

In the middle of a song

Or a sunrise

Or the smile of an innocent child.

There's nothing

Substantial

That we can grasp anyway,

So why not

Tear apart the curtains

That have kept us asleep

So long,

And let the daylight in,

Airing out all the hidden corners,

And allowing ourselves

To breathe again

At last.

Is there any other choice now,

But to get

Completely real,

And take the vow

Of the Compassionate One,

The Bodhisattva,

Who says:

"For the benefit of all sentient beings.

As long as space remains,

As long as sentient beings remain,

Until then, may I too remain

And dispel the miseries of the world.

Like the great earth and the other elements,

Enduring as the sky itself endures,

For the boundless multitude of living beings,

May I be the ground and vessel of their life.

Thus, for every single thing that lives,

In number like the boundless reaches of the sky,

May I be their sustenance and nourishment

Until they pass beyond the bounds of suffering"

And so may it be,

That we all

Finally

Come home.

7.16.13

There's this new sensation

Of Earth Energy

Rising in spirals

To meet

Sun/Star/Moon Energy

That's flowing down

From above.

They twine about each other

In the heart

And make magic

Elixirs

That pour out again,

In beautiful patterns

Of light

Through all the channels

And circuits

And centers of power

In this body

And beyond,

To bless the world

With abundant

Nectars

Of love.

From wild formless feelings

To pinpointed actions

Of generosity,

We move

Like a Brandenburg Concerto-

Crescendo, decrescendo,

Layers of harmony

And counterpoint

Building

To an ecstatic architecture

Of praise

To the divine within

The mundane.

Here, just now–

Let's hold our fingers

In the rays of this

Crystal prism

And let the Light

Dance through our souls

To infinity.

7.17.13

Without

Even the vaguest

Notion

Of what is going to happen,

Can we just sit

With uncertainty?

Just drop this

Incessant need

To control the process

Or preview the outcome

And allow our souls to trust.

How spacious our hearts and minds,

Bodies and the world itself

Suddenly become!

Sitting on the summit

With endless views

To the horizon,

The sweet, fresh wind

Blowing right through us,

And carrying away

Any last effort

At analysis.

Let's just rest

Here for a long breath,

Feeling the effervescence

Of True Presence

Bubbling up

Through our beings,

And washing us

So gently,

Completely

Clean.

7.18.13

We can rest now,

In the warm encompassing arms

Of the Mother's magnetic embrace,

And allow ourselves

To be held,

Cherished and nurtured

By all of nature's

Abundantly apparent

Generosity.

And in this time,

The vital imperative

Would be then,

To share this generosity

With every wounded woman,

Every abandoned child, or unloved man-

To be wild and uninhibited

In our compassion,

To hold nothing back

In the nakedness of our

Open hearts;

To feel so deeply

And exquisitely

The pain of each other's,

And of our own conditioned existence-

That we're willing to do whatever

Is needed

To alleviate the suffering

Of this World.

Take a breath with me now,

And we'll all hold hands

And watch together-

The sun as it sets

And the moon as She rises.

7.20.13

Silver the sky,

And the water's reflection,

And the sound of

Wind-blown bells

At midnight.

The Moon

Dances Her Slow

Exotic waltz

Across the heavens,

And we respond

Like the tides,

Pulled out of ourselves–

Far from shore,

Then returned,

Inexorably

To the gritty sandiness

On this little ledge of land.

We feel

The exfoliation

Of our skin,

Outside

And in-

The deeper places

Letting go with reluctance

Of their known

Safety zones

Of long-lost paradigms

And outmoded manners of speech.

Quiet remains

The master of breath,

And as we respond

To the silent request-

Heartbeat

Resting;

Mind and body

Still,

At last-

We realize

This gentle wisdom,

And become

Translucent,

Silver

Mirrors

Of the Moon.

7.21.13

Breathing in through every pore

Till the center

Is so full of light

That the old structure dissolves

And all that's left

Is this shimmering

Shakti dakini,

Dancing right through me,

And reshaping the universe

With the wisdom

Of Her gaze.

Deep discernment

Allows the jewel rays

Of a thousand scintillating gems

To illuminate

And penetrate

Every known reality,

Until all that's left

Is a pile of colored thread

On the threshing floor

Of the mind.

Following feelings,

Every root has been explored

And compassionately pulled

From its safe enclosure,

And metamorphosed

Into food

For the free,

Wild energy

That builds now,

Spiraling up the tree,

And releasing radiance

Like a flock of shining,

Celebrating,

Sunlit doves

Flying home

Through the great wide

Blue and limitless sky.

7.23.13

Photo Credit: Don V Lax

Truth

In every form

Is information

Arriving from every direction

And allowing us the delicious opportunity

Of choosing what flavor

Will nourish our souls

And consequently

What part

Of the great rainbow spectrum

We would like to emit

In that moment.

This dance is happening continuously,

In countless dimensions,

With our heart at the center,

And our clear intention

Is the musician

Effortlessly weaving

A million particles of light

Into one great diaphanous

Symphony of beauty

For all to share.

Every being, a vital strand

In the spinning thread

That grows like galaxies

From the wheel

Of infinite wisdom-

And as we reflect each other,

A million trillion and more

Stars that sparkle and shine

Through the depths

Of the silken night.

7.24.13

A message arrived

Clearly stating:

The struggle has ended...

It's time to be letting

The inner wisdom

Dance

With the world

As it is,

And know:

Each miniscule

Perfection of beauty

That spontaneously arises

From the heart

Is a gift from,

And back to

The Universe

Herself.

7.25.13

Could we possibly

Take a day

To leave behind

The language

In our minds?

All the neural structures

Paved by lifetimes of categorizing

And judging...

Of for and against,

Good, bad and indifferent...

Suddenly

All the windows would be

Wide open

And a sweetly scented

Summer breeze

Would blow through

The airy, open space that was,

Just moments before,

So cluttered

And claustrophobic.

Our brains would become

The magical sense organs

Of a sentient world,

Totally psychic,

Empathic,

Sensitive to everything

And just naturally

Feeling the Beauty

And compassion

Arising from our own

Hearts.

And brilliant?

Einstein would be proud!

Nothing to keep

Full function

From streaming

All available awareness

And pinpointed concentration

To any unfolding experience.

Let's go for a swim

With a hundred wild

And joyous dolphins

And let them teach us

The language

Of the Dreamtime...

No words-

Just beautiful images

Projected

On waves

Of song.

7.26.13

So fine,

The multicolored thread

With which we embroider

This pattern

Of pure attention.

With a needle point

Measured in nano-particles,

We pierce the fabric

Of our sense-net surroundings,

And stitch fractal spirals

Of quantum wave-forms

To piece together

A coherent whole.

The bodhisattva

Listens with care

To 9 billion voices

Crying at once for compassion-

And, without denying a single teardrop,

Remains calm, clear and loving

In the eye at the center

Of the storm.

Owning nothing

And open to everything,

All that is needed

For each unfolding moment

Arises effortlessly

And heals

The wounds of the World.

7.27.13

Would you care to join me

As I rest my forehead

On the knee

Of the

Compassionate One?

We will request

That She kindly

Remove

All obstacles

Between ourselves

And total liberation...

And in Her Presence,

We will disrobe

Completely, and forever

Leaving behind

These fragmented attempts

At holding reality at bay

With awkward fantasies

Of style and self-importance.

Returned to our crystalline essence

In the Radiance of Her gaze-

We reflect and refract

A million spectrums of light

Beyond anything we ever dreamed,

And so absorbed

By the beauty of that music,

Our bodies turn

In ecstatic communion

With our one Great Soul,

And we Dance.

7.28.13

Hold gently

The little things

That cross your palm

In beauty.

Whisper to them

Softly,

And call them

By their names.

Take a small portion

Of time,

To dwell outside

Of space-

And relocate your mind

Inside your heart.

For here is where

The tiniest of miracles

Grows large

Enough to encompass

Star-systems...

And where a simple act of generosity

Can affect the outcome

Of ancient history.

This tender,

Vulnerable organ

In the center of your being

Is the key to every mystery-

And the sound of this rhythm-

This primal root-tone

Is the magic incantation

That opens the gateway

To eternity.

7.29.13

How easy it is

To dance in the rain

And be cleansed once again

Of every last vestige

That remains

Of adversity.

This day

We entered the dimension

Of gladness,

And felt lifetimes of sadness

Dissolve like dreams

Of lost harmonies

And resolve

Into a sonata

So sweet

That now,

Sunshine sparkles

Like gold flecks

In blue eyes,

And every spiral

Strand of DNA

Is singing

With new light;

Welcoming home

The wandering soul-

So long a stranger

In such a strange world...

This body open,

At last completely

Ready to receive

Its own

Divine nature.

7.30.13

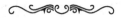

Morning sun

Brings light to our eyes.

Breathe it inside

And illuminate

Our entire

Interior.

Drop down now

To the womb of your being,

And experience

The complete connection

And comfort of resting,

Nestled in the arms

Of galaxies and nebulae

Who all love you

With the tenderness

Of the most compassionate

Grandmother.

So safe and nurtured,

Held and whole,

The tender sprout

Of your vulnerable heart

Can finally root

Into the rich earth below,

And grow, and grow

Till a thousand blossoms

With a fragrance way beyond

Even roses and jasmine and gardenias,

Bursting with the radiance

Of every imaginable precious jewel,

Bloom

For the benefit

Of all beings everywhere...

And we bow,

In overwhelming gratitude.

8.1.13

Last rays

Of this day's

Setting sun

Fill the lapis blue sky

With dancing geometries

Of such exquisite perfection

That our souls are silenced

In awe and wonder

And the music of the moment

Simply sings

Through our entire

Being.

Nothing can reproduce

This singular event-

We can only open to its essence-

And by this receptive loving,

Become one with the beautiful song.

A million sunsets

Might be remembered

Or forgotten

But if we live this miracle

In fullness

It will be

The only one

For this eternal moment.

8.2.13

Quietly sensing

The world

Without thought

Or preconception-

The mind becomes tactile

And all experience

A pleasure of perception.

Here we can welcome

Every heart that we've broken

And every injury we've been done,

Feeling everything,

Forgiving everything,

Accepting everything-

With love and compassion

Until, at last-

Every iota of our personality

From every lifetime

In every dimension

Has been cleansed...

Not even the vaguest impulse

To push or pull

On the universe

Remains.

Just this vast willingness

To be here-

Exactly here where

We find ourselves in this

Present moment-

And completely alert,

Ready to be

Exactly appropriate

For whatever

Arises.

8.3.13

Sit naked on the sand by the sea,

And feel the Earth Herself

Supporting every cell

Of your being-

Open wide from root to crown

And receive the rising tide

Flowing in from the sun,

Moon and stars

In their dance

With this Blue planet

Of ours.

In gratitude for these gifts,

Let us pray

That all oceans,

Rivers, lakes and streams everywhere

Return to their original

Pristine purity,

And that all beings

Be healed and find

Their own divinity.

Holding this prayer

In our hearts,

And moving within that rhythm,

Let us walk slowly

Into the welcoming water,

And swim

Into the temple

Of light.

8.4.13

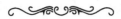

Enter with attention

The dimension

Of beauty-

We walk wakefully,

With gentle care,

And note

The refinement

Of each aspect

Of awareness...

Feeling the fullness

Of passionate care

For every atom

In this existence,

How can we do other

Than allow

The Goddess to express

Through us

Her Great Compassion

For all?

She has always been

The guiding hand,

The Light,

The window,

And the doorway

To return,

After so many lifetimes,

To our true heart's

Desire and

Destiny.

8.5.13

The absolute

Pleasure of pure presence

Tingles in every part

Of this body-

Released

From lifetimes

Of holding

Every imaginable hurt,

We are free to experience

The soul's brilliance

And curiosity,

And to explore

The delicious opportunities

Presented by life

In this wondrous form.

The mind has become

A sense organ

For bliss—

Following pathways

Of light, dark, and a million colored

Moonbeams

To discover

The full anatomy

Of each moment—

The full extent

Of each breath,

And the full potential

Of all the universes

And their lovers

Meeting in full tantric union

In the center

Of our own hearts.

8.6.13

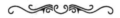

We are being asked to evolve

At accelerated velocity-

And to handle energy

Of massive magnitude...

A galactic storm,

A solar wild fire,

A radioactive world,

And a human population

In such mental, emotional and physical

Distress

That the average person seems

Completely disconnected

From True Reality.

So now what

Is a Bodhisattva to do?

Baby, all I want to do is dance-

Dance with the energies

In all their manifestations,

Sing wild harmonies

With every music that emerges

From any situation.

Joyously swim

Like a glorious pod of dolphins

Into the eye of everything

That appears,

And with the tenderness

And infinite attention

Of the Goddess of Compassion,

Give all that we have

With such openhearted generosity

That all beings

Are instantly

Healed.

8.7.13

This humming in our heads,

Like a hive of honey bees:

A gentle, persistent

Mantra of remembrance,

Calling us

Again and again,

Repeatedly

Back behind the curtain;

Behind the mind,

And the thoughts, the emotions,

(The constant projection

outwards...)

Back here, where we are

Quiet and free-

Deep in the deepest,

High in the highest,

Completely alone,

And totally merged,

One with everyone and everything.

Yes, this untamed, melodious

Harmonic series

Rising from infrared to ultraviolet

Through every echoing

Hall of the Great Temple

We call our Body–

Resounding outward,

Beyond the stratosphere,

To kiss the stars and planets

And let all sentience

In every realm

Return

To the one

True song.

8.8.13

If we were

To turn ourselves

Inside out,

Like a figure eight

Moving through

All the possible permutations

Of our own spiritual

Topography...

What wonders and magic

Might we then find,

To reveal the full extension

Of our multi-dimensional

Nature!

Like sunlight and shadow,

Dancing across the mirror glass

Of a morning sea's

Crystal blue reflection,

We orbit and spin,

Weaving elliptical spirals

Through this space and time...

Ripples and waves

Respond to our intention,

And new realities are born

From our emerging dreams.

Let us, then,

Take infinite care

With all that we encounter,

And let our lives

Be a blessing

To every being that enters

The abode of our awareness.

8.9.13

A blessing of rain

Brings forth the scent

Of night-blooming jasmine,

And washes away

All the accumulated dust of the day.

This sweet fresh feeling

Of sky-water on skin

Leaves us tingling

With awakened senses

And alive with the brilliant clarity

Of unborn beauty.

Empty of agendas, open to infinity,

We rest

In complete awareness and readiness

For the universe

And her boundless generosity.

8.10.13

Into sweet silence

Of deepest night,

A thousand stars

Fall

In ecstasies

Of self-sacrifice.

Not reacting

To any outer oppression,

Nor responding

To any need

For grand display-

They're simply

Available at the appropriate

Moment for this

Annual extravaganza

Of random beauty.

Let's never hide

From the opportunity

To be that way-

Ready, willing and able

For the Universe

To call us into service

To fulfill

Whatever grand design

She might have

At any given moment.

8.11.13

Exploring

Being porous

Is the experiment

For today.

We're opening

Our skin and all

Our senses

To allow everything

And everyone

Free passage,

Welcome,

With a smile...

The world

Is so intensely

Interesting

When we no longer

Have any labels

For anything...

The taste of seawater

As we ride the swell

Upside down

And backwards

Sparkles like the silver

Sunlight that's filtering

Through a thousand

Liquid facets

To fill this temple

In the location formerly known

As "the brain"

With rainbows...

8.12.13

If we could

Return to the womb

For a while

And remember that

Fluid condition

Of being

Merged with the Mother-

So loved,

So held and nourished

And connected in every way

With everything...

Would we then

Live our lives

Free of distortion and disconnection,

Touching the world

With senses awake and aware,

And amazed by the beauty of all?

So fragile and fresh,

So ready for fulfillment,

We emerge into

Epiphanies of tenderness

And grace.

Could we now

Become together

A humanity so caring,

So compassionate,

That every mother and child

Would feel so blessed

And free

And safe forever.

8.13.13

Deep green like velvet moss,

Damp by a sweet clear spring

Divinely sings

The crystal tones

Of water so pure

That your heart aches

With the very beauty of its essence.

Let's lay our bodies down right here

And unwind all the way

Back to the source

Of our existence.

Let's allow our souls

To sink right through our cells

And touch the primal heart of things.

And with that contact,

That reconnection,

That long-lost love...

We find ourselves

Suffused with softness,

Yet strong with the power

Of ultimate trust,

And enthusiastic

With the energy

That fuels entire universes

Of creative potential.

Rest now

In this verdant magic,

And let the healing happen

For all who thirst or sorrow

In this entire world.

8.14.13

We are all called now

To stand together

In the heart

Of the Central Sun.

The Diamond Fire

Is bringing us home

To burn in Her embrace

Every last trace of anything

That could keep us

From the present journey

Of ascension.

There is no more room

For doubt–

The time is now to trust

That we have been prepared

For this:

To Really Feel

Our Full Presence

Here in our bodies

On this wounded planet,

Holding it all

In the container of love,

And opening all the way

Through the Earth,

Into the Sun-

And with that connection,

Resume our true identity

As an awakened

Galactic Soul.

8.16.13

We're learning

To live

Like a lovesong

For the soul-

A melody so yearning,

So full of sweetness

And sorrow,

That even the most wayward

Of wandering spirits

Could not help

But heed

The call.

And when She

Returns to the Temple,

Oh what a celebration we have prepared!

All the stars and planets

Will come dancing-

Great hearts of galaxies

Will beat like a million drums...

Oceans will rise, Waters will fall,

And all the Gods and Goddesses

Will Rejoice.

But most of all-

Without even

Making a sound,

This body will melt

To receive Her home,

And all the lifetimes of longing

Will be healed

When she blesses his brow

With a kiss.

8.17.13

A lake full of galaxies,

A sky full of stars,

Vision gazing on and on

Into depths of infinity...

Opening deeper and wider

Till heart aches from everything;

The world- pain, beauty,

Entropy/

Perfection-

And this radiance surrounding us

In a sphere of sparkling light,

Is shot across

By a streak of dying luminescence-

Like a whole lifetime going by

In one rhapsodic

Moment.

Let's live like that-

Fearless

In our full power,

Nothing held back-

Blazing our joy

Across the universe.

8/20/09

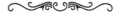

Photo Credit: Desiree' K. DallaGuardia

Table of Contents